WANDERLUST

Journal for Travel lovers

DEDICATION

Dedicated to my Mother who has gave me powerful wings to fly.

ACKNOWLEDGMENTS

I would like to thank my friends for supporting this project and for their valuable feedback. In special to Chris, Esteban, John, Andrea y Sandra.
And also a big thanks to my family which have taught me to live in reflexive mode.

CONTENTS

- Before Travelling

- While Travelling

- Back from Travelling

WANDERLUST

WANDERLUST
Journal for Travel lovers

WANDERLUST

If FOUND

Please return it to

Name:

Address:

Phone number:

Email address:

TRAVEL
IS FOOD
FOR THE
SOUL

WANDERLUST

WANDERLUST

The term originates from the German words wandern (to hike) and Lust (desire).
English occurred in 18th century as a reflection of what was then seen as a characteristically German predilection for wandering.

In modern German, the use of the word Wanderlust is less common, having been replaced by Fernweh (lit. "farsickness"), coined as an antonym to Heimweh ("homesickness").
Wanderlust is the intense urge for self-development by experiencing the unknown, confronting unforeseen challenges, getting to know unfamiliar cultures, ways of life and behaviours.

WHAT IS TO TRAVEL?

When we travel, we move along distance and time, between two different points.

Etymology

The first known word use was in the 14th century. The word "travel" may originate from the Old French which means to work strenuously.

The origin of the word reflects the extreme difficulty of travel in ancient times.

Even though today it is easier to travel, we are used to travel hurriedly. We are used to follow the masses and to do what everyone tells us to do. This book, suggests ways to make a pause and contemplate details, and motivates us to write down all our thoughts.

25 GREAT REASONS
TO TRAVEL

Some people say we travel only for two reasons,

- either to escape from something
- or to look for something new.

But there are more reasons.

1. Travel is to leave the beaten path
2. Travel is opening wounds, so then the sun can heal them
3. Travel gives us an excuse to learn a new language.
4. Travel is open the door to the unconscious memories
5. Travel makes us rethink stereotypes.
6. Travel is to convert the lack of Wifi in the possibility of looking into the eyes of those who are travelling with you

7. Travel makes us believe in the kindness of strangers.
8. Travel is to leave all the excuses at home
9. Travel is to expand our tolerance
10. Travel makes it okay not to fit in
11. Travel gives us the opportunity to start from scratch
12. Travel makes us remove the autopilot with which we drive our lives
13. Travel makes us vulnerable
14. Travel is to reinvent ourselves
15. Travel makes us to be friends of strangers
16. Travel is to get lost to finally find with anyone else but ourselves
17. Travel makes us do crazy things
18. Travel is like jumping from stone to stone the river of life. Where every stone are the trips we have done, and the river flowing, our daily lives
19. Travel makes us enjoy discomfort

20. Travel makes us appreciate home

21. Travel is a panacea

What are the reasons why I Travel?

22. ...

23. ...

24. ...

25. ...

THE THREE STAGES OF A TRIP

TRAVEL IS PURE INSPIRATION

The word inspiration comes from the Latin word "inspiratio", inspiration is the process on which outside air enters the lungs and promotes thoughts in the mind

In Greek thought, inspiration meant that the artist would go into ecstasy. It was the figure of the muse that was considered to be the goddess who "carried" the artists to perform their different jobs.

Life begins with an inspiration, and when life itself expires, it does so with an exhalation. This trip is my inspiration.

BEFORE TRAVELLING BACK

W?

Before starting my trip, I'll define the 5 "W":

What? (Do I want to learn from this trip)

When? (Do I travel?)

Where? (Do I go?)

Why? (Do I travel?)

How? (Will I do it?)

WANDERLUST

ONLY WHAT I NEED

I'm Taking
what I need

for

This Trip

Courage | Freedom | Hope | Patience | Strength | Open mind | ...

WANDERLUST

THINGS TO DO BEFORE LEAVING

I should not forget to:

Water the plants

Enable the "out the office notification"

-
-
-
-
-
-
-
-

WANDERLUST

PACKING LIST

> The size of the luggage = the size of the fears

Here are the things I would like to take with me:

-
-
-
-
-
-
-
-
-
-
-

- •
- •
- •
- •
- •
- •
- •
- •
- •
- •
- •
- •
- •

And now I will remove 3 things that I might not need

MY ITINERARY

Day	Flight	Hotel	To visit

Day	City	Hotel	To visit

Day	City	Hotel	to visit

THANKS!

The most powerful word: thanks!

How to say it in 40 different languages

AFRIKAANS — dankie

ALBANIAN — faleminderit

ARABIC — shukran

BULGARIAN — благодаря / blagodaria

CATALAN — gràcies (GRAH-syuhs)

CANTONESE — Mˋh'gōi

CROATIAN — hvala (HVAH-lah)

CZECH — děkuji (Dyekooyih)

DANISH — tak (tahg)

DUTCH — dank u

ESTONIAN — tänan (TA-nahn)

FINNISH — kiitos (KEE-tohss)

FRENCH — merci

GERMAN — danke

GREEK — ευχαριστώ (ef-hah-rees-TOH)

HAWAIIAN — mahalo (ma-HA-lo)

HEBREW — תודה / todah (toh-DAH)

HINDI — dhanyavād / shukriya

HUNGARIAN — köszönöm (KØ-sø-nøm)

INDONESIAN — terima kasih (tuh-REE-mah KAH-see)

ITALIAN — grazie (GRAHT-tsyeh)

JAPANESE — arigatô (ah-ree-GAH-toh)

KOREAN – 감사합니다 (gamsahamnida)

LATVIAN – paldies (PUHL-dyehs)

LEBANESE – choukrane

LITHUANIAN – ačiū (AH-choo)

MACEDONIAN – **Благодарам** / blagodaram (blah-GOH-dah-rahm)

MALAY – terima kasih (TREE-muh KAH-seh)

MANDARIN – Xièxiè

NORWEGIAN – takk

POLISH – dziękuję (Jenkoo-yen)

PORTUGUESE – obrigado [masculine] / obrigada [feminine] (oh-bree-

ROMANIAN – mulţumesc (mool-tzoo-MESK)

RUSSIAN – **спасибо** (spuh-SEE-buh)

SERBIAN – хвала / hvala (HVAH-lah)

SLOVAK – Ďakujem (JAH-koo-yehm)

SLOVENIAN – hvala (HVAA-lah)

SPANISH – gracias (GRAH-syahs)

SWEDISH – tack

THAI – kop khun

TURKISH – teşekkür ederim (teh shek uer eh der eem)

WORRIES OUT

What I should not be worried about
(but sometimes worries me...!)?

UTOPIA

An imagined place or state of things in which everything is perfect.
The truth is that, perfection is found also in the mistakes, in the disorder, in the imperfection.

MY UTOPIC TRIP WOULD BE

BEFORE   TRAVELLING   BACK

A LIFE EACH DAY

I'll bring a candy for each day of the trip.
Every morning I'll eat one, and it will make
me to be conscious of maximizing my day.
This day will never ever come back.
I plan to make today a special day doing the
following:

-
-
-
-
-

UBIQUITY

Is the capacity of being everywhere, at the same time; being omnipresent.
This is impossible.
In this trip I want to only be here.

I'll do that by:

✓ focusing on each thing I do.

✓ Turning off my cell phone as much as I can.

✓ ...

✓ ...

✓ ...

✓ ...

RECORD OF EXPENSES

Day	Flight	Mobility	Food		Total

Day	Flight	Mobility	Food		Total

Day	Flight	Mobility	Food		Total

COMFORT ZONE

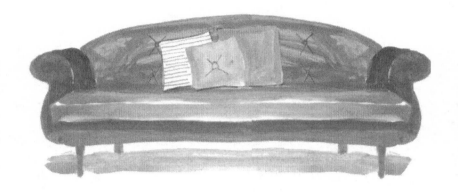

In order to leave my comfort zone, today I'll try to do something I have never done before and that is:

DAILY MOOD RECORD

TODAY I FEEL:

Day																			
Anxious																			
Calm																				
Content																			
Crappy																				
Crazy																				
Curious																				
Envious																				
Excited																				
Grateful																				
Grumpy																				
Guilty																				
Happy																				
Hopeful																				
Hot																				
Hungry																				
Hyper																				
Lonely																				
Loved																				
Mad																				
Peaceful																				
Relaxed																				
Sad																				

Day																			
Satisfied																			
Shocked																			
Thankful																			
Tired																			
Touched																			

TAKING A STARS WALK
I'm drawing here the position of stars I see
tonight in the sky

SERENDIPITOUS MOMENTS

Serendipity is an unexpected discovery when we are seeking something different.
The word emerged in 1700 from a Persian fairy tale, which takes place on an island called "Serendip", in which the protagonists solved all their problems through coincidences.
What is my Serendipitous moment in this trip?

FOOD

My favorite dishes in this trip are:

EPIPHANY

From the ancient Greek is an experience of sudden and striking realization. It happens when an enlightening realization allows a problem to be understood from a new and deeper perspective. Epiphanies can come in many different forms, and often are generated by a complex combination of experience, memory, knowledge, predisposition and context. In an epiphany, we see the entire answer to a complex problem.

Ways to have an epiphany:

- Interaction with different people, with different perspectives.
- Trying different activities, which have never been tried before.
- Meditating and relax.
- Choosing roads never before taken.

My epiphany of this trip is:

ROUTINE

A repeated formula, a predictable response, unimaginative processes.
The Routine tells us when to eat, to sleep and to dream.
Travel helps us to dream anytime.

Today I will leave the beaten path by doing this::

✓ ...

✓ ...

✓ ...

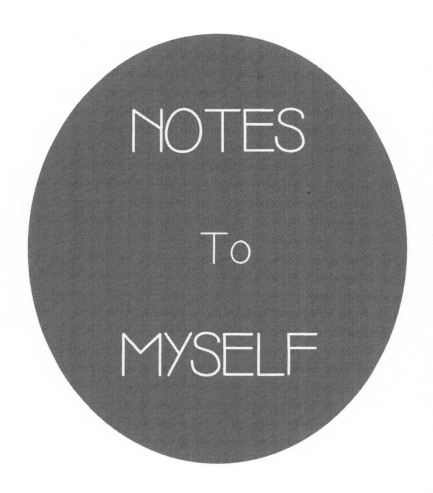

NOTES

To

MYSELF

When we travel we stop being who we are to become being who we want to be.

WANDERLUST

"The world is a book, and those who do not travel read only a page." Saint Augustine

WANDERLUST

"For once you have tasted flight you will walk the earth with your eyes turned skywards, for there you have been and there you will long to return." Leonardo da Vinci

WANDERLUST

"We wander for distraction, but we travel for fulfillment." Hilaire Belloc

WANDERLUST

"Own only what you can always carry with you: know languages, know countries, know people. Let your memory be your travel bag." Aleksandr Solzhenitsyn

WANDERLUST

"*To travel is to take a journey into yourself.*" Danny Kaye

WANDERLUST

"The traveler sees what he sees, the tourist sees what he has come to see." Gilbert K. Chesterton

WANDERLUST

"Discovery consists not in seeking new lands, but in seeing with new eyes." Marcel Proust

WANDERLUST

"Travel far enough, you meet yourself." David Mitchell

WANDERLUST

"It is better to travel well than to arrive." Buddha

WANDERLUST

"To travel is to discover that everyone is wrong about other countries." Aldous Huxley

WANDERLUST

"Tourists don't know where they've been, travelers don't know where they're going." Paul Theroux

WANDERLUST

"I never travel without my diary. One should always have something sensational to read in the train." Oscar Wilde

WANDERLUST

"*Travel - it leaves you speechless, then turns you into a storyteller.*" *Ibn Battuta*

WANDERLUST

"Twenty years from now you will be more disappointed by the things you didn't do than by the ones you did do." Mark Twain

WANDERLUST

"One's destination is never a place, but a new way of seeing things." Henry Miller

WANDERLUST

"It is not down in any map; true places never are." Herman Melville

WANDERLUST

> "Not all those who wander are lost." J.R.R. Tolkien

WANDERLUST

"He who would travel happily must travel light." Antoine de St. Exupery

WANDERLUST

"*People don't take trips, trips take people.*" John Steinbeck

WANDERLUST

"When overseas you learn more about your own country, than you do the place you're visiting."
Clint Borgen

WANDERLUST

"Do not go where the path may lead, go instead where there is no path and leave a trail." Ralph Waldo Emerson

WANDERLUST

"Travel is the only thing you buy that makes you richer."
Anonymous

WANDERLUST

"The man who goes alone can start today; but he who travels with another must wait till that other is ready." Henry David Thoreau

WANDERLUST

"We travel not to escape life, but for life not to escape us."
Anonymous

WANDERLUST

"*Like all great travelers, I have seen more than I remember, and remember more than I have seen.*" Benjamin Disraeli

WANDERLUST

WANDERLUST

WANDERLUST

WANDERLUST

WANDERLUST

WANDERLUST

WANDERLUST

WANDERLUST

WONDERFUL PEOPLE
I MET ON THIS TRIP

Name:

Email:

Country:

He / She Made my trip special because...

Name:

Email:

Country:

He / She Made my trip special because...

Name:

Email:

Country:

He / She Made my trip special because...

HOME

MY TAKEAWAY OF THIS TRIP:

I have learned.....

For next trip I would avoid.....

What I liked the most.....

COUNTRIES I HAVE VISITED

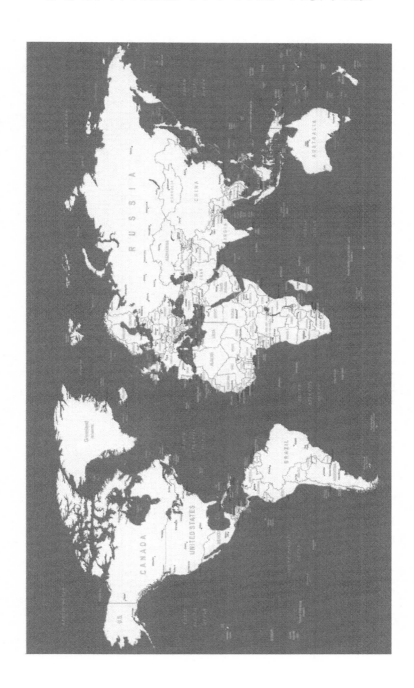

PICTURES
OF MY BEST MOMENTS

WANDERLUST

WANDERLUST

WANDERLUST

No End

Now It is the right time to start dreaming about a new journey

It is time to feel again WANDERLUST

WANDERLUST

Made in the USA
San Bernardino, CA
05 December 2016